THE COUNTRY CRAFT SERIES

DRIED
FLOWERS
& HERBS

THE COUNTRY CRAFT SERIES

DRIED FLOWERS & HERBS

CRESCENT BOOKS
NEW YORK • AVENEL, NEW JERSEY

This 1994 edition published by Crescent Books,
distributed by Random House Value Publishing, Inc.,
40 Engelhard Avenue, Avenel, New Jersey 07001.

Random House
New York • Toronto • London • Sydney • Auckland

First published in 1992
Reprinted in 1993
Reprinted in 1994

© Copyright Harlaxton Publishing Ltd
© Copyright design Harlaxton Publishing Ltd

Publishing Manager: Robin Burgess
Project Coordinator: Lynn Bryan
Project assistant: Jenny Johnson
Editor: Dulcie Andrews
Illustrator: Carol Ohlbach
Photographer: Andrew Elton
Designer: Kathie Baxter Smith
Typeset in the U.K. by Seller's
Produced in Singapore by Imago

Title: Country Crafts Series: Dried Flowers & Herbs
ISBN: 0 517 10253 6

CONTENTS

INTRODUCTION

The popularity of creating a beautiful craft by hand is increasing among people of all age groups.

Through this Country Craft series, it is our hope that you will find satisfaction and enjoyment in learning a new skill. In this case, that of drying flowers and herbs. Dried flowers conjure up images of a relaxed way of life and also add color and texture to any room in the house throughout the year.

Drying flowers and herbs is a straightforward and rewarding pastime, as you will discover.

Opposite: A mass of dried blooms creates a focal point in any room of the house.

GETTING STARTED

DRIED FLOWERS AND HERBS have been used as decorations throughout the home from the beginning of civilization. The process of drying flowers retains their beauty; with herbs, drying also retains flavor.

The art of drying flowers and herbs is thousands of years old. Many people have memories of the faint fragrance of a small sachet of lavender discovered while searching for treasures in grandmother's closet.

Ancient civilizations used the fragrances of dried flowers and herbs to perfume rooms. Rose petals were scattered on table tops; bunches of mixed dried flowers were hung from rafters or placed strategically around in vases and bowls. Leaves and flowers with long-lasting fragrances were often left in drawers and closets to rid clothes of musty smells.

Aromatic bunches of dried flowers and leaves were popular in Europe during the 17th century, mainly to ward off the ghastly smells associated with the plague.

The British embraced the craft wholeheartedly during the Victorian era, decorating their living areas with dried arrangements and their closets with perfumed sachets.

Interior decorating fashion has come full circle. In the late 20th century, with the current yearning for the traditions associated with a country lifestyle, dried flowers are seen in both town and country homes. The style of arrangement has changed, but the flowers are the same.

What is a dried flower? It is one which has either been air-dried or treated with a chemical desiccant and sand, or with glycerine to make it last a long time after it has bloomed. Choosing which flowers and herbs to dry for display, to make into a beautiful gift for a friend or, in the case of herbs, to store for later use as flavoring in dishes is a personal matter, but it is best to be guided by which plants are most suited for such treatment.

Air-drying is the easiest and most effective method. The ideal plants include statice, strawflowers, roses, larkspur, delphinium, saxifrage, baby's breath, and mimosa, plus grasses, seed heads and leaves.

Chemical desiccants and sand are also used to draw out moisture from plant material. By this method, plants retain much of their natural color, but the end product can be brittle. Desiccants are particularly good for roses, peonies, Christmas roses, lilies, orchids, tulips and zinnias. Glycerine is used to replace moisture in leaves and flowers so that the plant remains fairly supple.

Once you have thought carefully about which method you will use, decide which

Opposite: A small bunch wrapped with a gingham fabric bow makes a pretty gift for someone special.

Pine cones can be used to great effect once dried. This Christmas arrangement is neatly balanced by the wreath placed in the center, behind the two cone trees.

color grouping you prefer and select different types of flowers that are in harmony with this theme. It is important to follow your instinct and have confidence in your creative ability. Remember that handling flowers and herbs requires a gentle touch and patience.

For Christmas, a mixture of dried material in a contemporary style. The country colors are the most important element of this arrangement. They were carefully chosen to complement the winter season. The glazed container completes the arrangement.

TOOLS AND MATERIALS

You will need a basic kit:
florist's shears
a sharp steel knife
twine

For wiring stems, you will need:
florist's shears
medium-gauge wire
fine rosewire
gutta-percha tape

For creating arrangements, you will need:
florist's shears
sharp steel knife
various blocks of styrofoam
roll of narrow cellophane tape
medium-gauge wire
dry moss

To sort out the flowers you have picked for drying, you will need a level bench top, either in a workroom, a greenhouse, the kitchen, or the laundryroom. Clear the area of superfluous items. Always work in a tidy area, and discard leftover blooms or branches as you go. This will leave you free to concentrate on the task at hand. Place each of the tools you need within easy reach. Some professionals like to use a small glue gun to insure dried decorations survive rough handling. Glue guns are avail-

able at most large stationery stores.

If you want to store flowers for later use, you will need a collection of flat, medium-sized, cardboard boxes, sheets of tissue paper and newspapers. Ask your local florist if you can buy the boxes in which their fresh flowers are delivered each day. They are excellent for storage.

For drying flowers you need a room where the air circulation and the temperature are both constant. In the kitchen, an old clothesline is perfect to hang bunches from. If you do not have one, then you can have one made by a handyperson; it is not an expensive item. For herbs, or for drying the heads and petals of flowers, use a drying tray. You can buy these at specialty stores, or make your own by stretching cheesecloth, nylon screen mesh or fine link chicken wire tightly over a rectangular wooden frame. If space is limited, use trays that can be stacked, remembering that air must be able to circulate freely between them.

For herbs that you want to keep for later use in cooking, you will need storage jars that seal tightly.

Once you have mastered the craft of drying plants, you may wish to color some of them. For this you will need to buy spray cans in the paint colors of your choice.

Flower heads dry well when hung through a chicken wire screen. If you cannot find one in a store, you can make one yourself using a wooden frame with fine chicken wire stretched across.

gutta-percha tape

dry foam

medium gauge stub wire

sticky tape

fine gauge stub wire

sharp steel knife

snips

roll of twine

block of dry foam

dry foam balls

rust moss

Yarrow growing in the wild.

STARTING WORK

THERE IS A GREAT range of plant material that can be collected for drying. A comprehensive chart, later in this chapter, details when to pick which plant.

Generally, it is best to pick flowers and herbs in summer. You will have to judge the right moment – ideally, just before the flowers or herbs reach their prime. Wait until mid-morning, when the dew has evaporated, then pick. At the beginning of summer pick saxifrage, early roses and *Alchemilla* (lady's mantle.) Later in the season is the time to pick yarrow, baby's breath, statice, straw-flowers and larkspur. Towards the end of summer, pick hydrangeas.

Fall is the right time to pick ripened seed heads. Watch carefully and when they have reached what you think is their best color, pick them immediately. Once the sap has gone they become lifeless and drop.

Pompon dahlias and sprays of goldenrod are best picked in the fall and hung to dry. Late hydrangeas can be picked then, too. You can hang-dry them, or arrange them in a vase with a small amount of water in the bottom, which will evaporate, leaving the stem brittle.

Grasses, cereals, reeds and rushes can also be picked. Lay them out carefully to dry. Some seed heads may need to be sprayed to insure they do not break. Use hairspray or a similar fixative. Dry these as quickly as possible.

Winter is the season to collect the type of branches and twigs that give structure and texture to dried arrangements. It is best to cut them when the sap is low, that is, when they feel dry. Pine cones should be open when you pick them up. Look for interesting shapes and try to find branches covered with moss. This adds textural variation.

If you do not have access to a well stocked yard (either your own or a friend's,) visit the local flower market early in the morning and have a good look around. Check that the flower heads are in pristine condition before you buy them; wilting flowers will produce unsatisfactory dried ones. Also, talk to your florist about the sorts of flowers that are best to dry for an arrangement.

HERBS

Ideally, pick fresh herbs from your yard in spring or summer and dry these for later use. Most people dry herbs to use as flavoring in cooking, but there are some long-stemmed herbs which are for dry-hanging in bunches – for example, lavender, any of the mints and southernwood.

Do not use hung herbs for flavoring food – they tend to get very dusty. However, they do look very attractive in the kitchen, or as part of other dried arrangements.

Strongly flavored herbs dried for culinary use should be kept away from other herbs to insure the flavors do not mix.

Herbs are valued for the minerals and

Above: A bunch of dried lavender.

vitamins they contain as well as for the flavor they add to food. Some herbs are known for their cleansing and healing properties. If you have a herb garden, then you are lucky in having a selection of these easily dried plants at your fingertips.

If you are planning a herb garden, plant French lavender, sage, parsley, basil, dwarf rosemary, oregano, tarragon, dill, thyme, sweet marjoram, common mint, eau de cologne mint, peppermint, lemon thyme, savory, cilantro, borage and fennel.

When you have collected the materials, do the drying almost immediately. Once you have sorted through, picked off damaged leaves, trimmed odd branches and stems, then you can start the preserving processes described in the following chapter. Flowers, branches full of leaves, and bunches of herbs left in a heap will soon rot.

Everlasting (Strawflowers) blooms are a colorful sight and easy to grow.

SUITABLE PLANTS FOR DRYING

Some of these plants may only be available from specialty suppliers.
Latin names have been given for easier identification,
since common names vary in different areas.

LATIN NAME	COMMON NAME	TIME TO PICK	PARTS TO USE
Acacia sp.	wattle, (tree-mimosa)	Spring	Flower head, leaf
Acanthus	bear's breeches	Summer	Flower spikes
Achillea sp.	yarrow, sneezewort	Spring	Flower head, leaf
Alchemilla mollis	lady's-mantle	Summer	Flower head, leaf
Alcea rosea	hollyhock	Summer	Seed heads
Amaranthus sp.	love-lies-bleeding	Summer	Seed head
Anaphalis sp.	pearly everlasting	Summer	Spray
Angelica archangelica	angelica	Summer	Culinary, potpourri
Anigozanthos sp.	kangaroo paw	Fall	Flower head
Anthemis nobilis	chamomile	Summer	Flower head
Arctotis sp.	African daisy	Summer	Flower head
Aruncus	goatsbeard	Spring	Flower head
Banksia sp.		Spring	Leaf
Betula pendula	silver birch	Winter	Spray
Callistemon sp.	bottle brush	Summer	Flower head
Centaurea cyanus sp.	cornflower	Summer	Flower head
Choisya ternata	Mexican orange blossom	Summer	Foliage
Chrysanthemum sp.	chrysanthemum	Fall	Flower head
Cimicifuga	bugbane	Summer	Seed heads

LATIN NAME	COMMON NAME	TIME TO PICK	PARTS TO USE
Clematis sp.	clematis	Fall	Seed head
Clematis vitalba	traveller's joy	Fall	Spray and seed head
Cortaderia selloana	pampas grass	Evergreen	Silky plumes
Cyperus papyrus	Egyptian paper rush	Summer	Seed head
Cytisus	broom	Summer	Branch flowers
Dahlia sp.	dahlia pompon	Summer	Flower head
Delphinium consolida	larkspur	Summer	Flower head
Dianthus sp.	pinks, carnations	Summer	Seed head
Digitalis sp.	foxglove	Summer	Seed heads
Dryandra formosa	golden dryandra	Spring	Flower head
Eryngium martimum	sea holly	Summer	Toothed bracts
Eucalyptus cinerea	gum tree	Fall	Leaf
Eucalyptus globulus	Tasmanian blue gum	Fall	Leaf, seed head
Fagus cuprea	copper beech	Summer	Spray, leaf
Fagus sylvatica	common beech	Summer	Spray, leaf
Garrya elliptica		Spring	Catkins
Gentiana	gentians	Summer	Sprigs
Grimmia pulvinata	bunmoss	Winter	Leaf
Gypsophila sp.	baby's breath	Summer	Flower head

LATIN NAME	COMMON NAME	TIME TO PICK	PARTS TO USE
Helichrysum sp.	everlasting or strawflower	Summer	Flower head
Hordeum jubatum	squirrel-tail grass	Fall	Grass seed head
Hordeum sp.	black-eared barley	Fall	Grass seed head
Hydrangea	hydrangea, inc. lacecaps	Fall	Flower head
Juncus sp.	bog rush	Fall	Seed head
Larix sp.	larch	Fall	Seed head
Lavendula angustifolia	old English lavender	Summer	Flower head
Leptospermum	tea-tree	Fall	Spray
Limonium sp.	statice, sea lavender	Summer	Flower head
Lunaria rediviva	honesty	Fall	Seed head
Mahonia aquifolium	Oregon grape	Spring	Racemes
Milium sp.	millet	Fall	Seed head
Moluccella laevis	bells of Ireland	Summer	Spray
Myrtus sp.	myrtle	Summer	Leaf
Myosotis sp.	forget-me-not	summer	Flower spray
Nigella damascena	love-in-a-mist	Summer	Seed head
Olearia sp	daisy bush tree aster	Summer	Seed head
Papaver sp.	poppies	Summer	Flower, seed head
Phleum pratense	timothy	Summer	Seed head
Phragmites	reed	Summer	Seed head
Physalis alkekengii	Chinese lanterns	Fall	Fruit pods
Pinus sp.	pine	Fall	Seed head, cone
Protea sp.	cape honey flower	Summer	Flower head

LATIN NAME	COMMON NAME	TIME TO PICK	PARTS TO USE
Ranculus acris	buttercup	Summer	Flower head
Rosa sp.	rose	Summer	Flower head
Salix myrsinites	willow	Fall	Leaf, catkins
Solidago canadensis	golden rod	Fall	Spray
Sphagnum sp.	sphagnum moss	Summer	Leaf
Stachys lantana	lamb's ear	Summer	Leaf

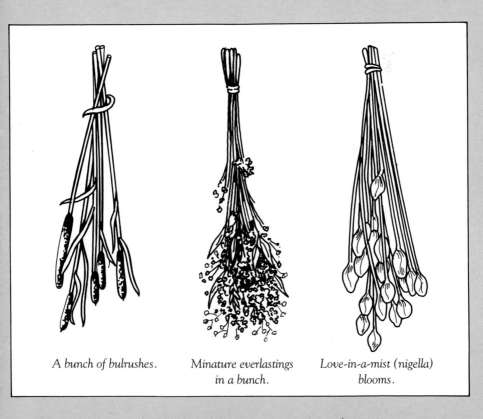

A bunch of bulrushes.

Minature everlastings
in a bunch.

Love-in-a-mist (nigella)
blooms.

Following page: A country kitchen is the perfect place to hang and air-dry herbs and flowers.

Lloyd Park

An unusual, modern, wall-hung arrangement of dried materials in the shape of a Christmas tree.

TECHNIQUES OF THE CRAFT

AIR-DRYING

The simplest and most popular method of drying plants and herbs is air-drying. All you need is a dry, cool room (where the temperature is constant), with good air circulation. Most flowers can be hung in bunches.

To hang, strip the first 4 inches of each stem and tie the flowers together with string. Bunch loosely and make sure there is enough air circulating around the plants or they will rot. Some plants can be dried lying flat, others can stand upright in a vase.

Grasses, fungi, twigs and bamboo are suitable for drying flat. Their leaves will shrink but they will keep their natural shape and color on the stem.

It is important to lay the plants on a surface which will absorb moisture – newspaper and posterboard are excellent. Leave a lot of space around the plants for air circulation.

There are two ways to dry plants standing upright in a vase. Some tall grasses and seed heads like pampas, dock, bulrushes and sea lavender dry well when just left in a dry and empty vase.

Hydrangea, mimosa, gypsophila and delphinium will dry better if stood in about 2 inches of water. The water evaporates (after being absorbed by the plant stem) and the

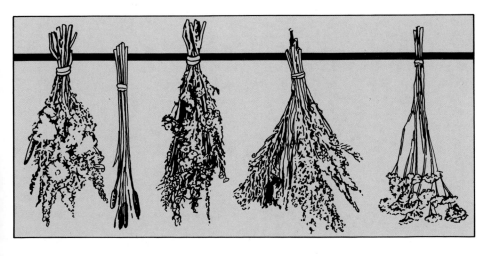

plant dries out.

You can also dry leaves and petals separately. Rose petals, lemon verbena, scented geraniums or whole flower heads without their stems will dry if they are placed in a single layer on a drying tray (see "Tools and Materials".)

The drying time for herbs and flowers varies from 2 to 10 days, depending upon the humidity and the amount of moisture in the leaves. Herbs sometimes take up to two weeks to dry.

Check herbs regularly, turning them over daily, until you feel they are crisp. When they are completely dry, place the herbs in an airtight container. Label the jar and store it in a dark closet.

If the weather is damp, try this alternative method, but do it with care. Place herbs or petals on a baking sheet and put them in the oven, at your oven's lowest temperature. It is best to leave the oven door open slightly. The faster the plants dry, the more fragrance and color they retain, especially the herbs.

If you have a microwave, place two sheets of paper towel on the turntable, spread out the leaves and petals on top and cover with two more paper towels. Set the microwave on high for 1 minute, although some herbs may take longer. Check frequently and as soon as they are crisp, place in a jar, label and store.

DRYING MOSS IN A BOX

All mosses dry well in a box. Lay the moss in a single layer on a mass of crumpled newspaper in a box. Pack it loosely so the air can circulate or the moss will rot. Dry sphagnum moss, lichen and selaginella can all be dried using this method.

CONES

Cones start drying while they are on the tree. Collect well-shaped cones from the ground and place them in a large basket or wooden bowl so that air can reach into the scales. Turn them occasionally and, when there is no moisture between scales, they are dry.

USING GLYCERINE

If you use glycerine to preserve plant leaves and other material, you will need to discover the advantages and disadvantages. With glycerine, the material remains supple, however, leaves and flowers change color and usually become a pale, dull, brown shade.

The method involves placing material in a mixture of glycerine and water. The plant absorbs the mixture and the water gradually evaporates, leaving the plant saturated with the glycerine. In preparation for this process, strip the end of the stem of leaves and cut the stem at a sharp angle. Hardwood stems should be split and hammered. A typical glycerine mixture consists of 40 percent glycerine to 60 percent hot water. Pour the mixture into a suitable vase to a depth of 4 inches and place the stems in vase. Keep this in a cool, dark place during absorption. Check the progress after a week.

To preserve good-sized leaves, place half-and-half glycerine/water mixture in a wide open bowl. Soak the leaves until the color changes completely, then remove from the mixture. Wash them in a mild detergent and lay them flat on sheets of newspaper to dry. These leaves will remain pliable for some time and a collection of leaves is handy when planning wreaths and other decorative items.

Ivy, magnolia, aspidistra and eucalyptus

leaves respond well to this method of preservation.

STORING DRIED MATERIAL

You can store dried material for several months without it deteriorating. The most attractive way to store bunches is by hanging them in a room, either from the ceiling or on a wall. Otherwise, you can store them in large, flat boxes. Make loose bunches and place in a box in layers. It is important to support fragile flower heads with crumpled tissue or newspaper. Delicate flower heads like roses, should be wrapped singly for better protection.

Do not mix preserved material with dried materials as the moisture will cause the former to rot. Store any boxed material in a dry place and, if you use a closet, make sure is well ventilated.

TO MAKE POTPOURRI

Dry potpourris can be made from any combination of colorful and fragrant flowers, herbs, and spices.

FOR COLOR	CORNFLOWERS, ROSES, MARIGOLDS, PANSIES
FOR FRAGRANCE	BERGAMOT, CHAMOMILE, CARNATIONS, VIOLETS, LAVENDER, JASMINE, MIMOSA, HONEYSUCKLE, PINKS
FOR SPICE	ALLSPICE, CARDAMOM, CINNAMON, CLOVES, GINGER, MACE
SCENTED LEAVES	BASIL, EUCALYPTUS, BAY, LEMON BALM, MYRTLE, ROSES, GERANIUMS, THYME, ROSEMARY

The way to make dry potpourri is simple. Mix dried, fragrant petals and leaves with herbs, spices, fixatives and oils and store in a sealed container for about six weeks. Then place the scented mixture into your favorite open bowls. The most common fixative is orris powder, available from a pharmacy, in a measure of 8 teaspoons per pound.

Experiment with different mixtures to find the fragrance you enjoy most of all. You can buy pure aromatic oils from specialty stores.

USING DESICCANTS

A desiccant is a drying agent. Silica gel, borax and sand, or a mixture of the three, are the most common agents used to absorb the water content from leaves and flowers. This method retains a freshness in form and color.

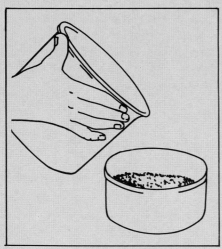

Fig. 1.

Fig. 2.

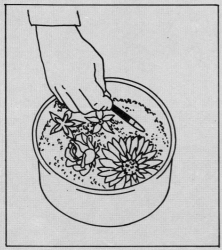

Fig. 3.

Fig. 4.

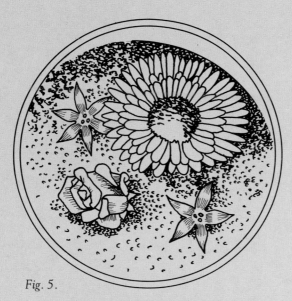

Fig. 5.

SILICA GEL

This dries material quickly and it can be used again and again. Pharmacies stock it in white crystals and as crystals with a color indicator. The latter are blue when dry and turn pink when they have absorbed water. It is important to grind the crystals to at least half their original size before use.

Fig. 1 Use a container that can be sealed tightly, for instance a cookie tin. Place a layer of crystals about 1/2 inch thick on the bottom of the container.

Fig. 2 Lay flower heads or leaves on top, adding more crystals.

Fig. 3 Make sure the crystals find their way between petals (use a small paintbrush to help them in) and cover the flowers and leaves completely.

Fig. 4 Seal the container.

Fig. 5 Open it after 2 days and it should be firm to touch. By this time the color indicator should have changed color. Remove plant material as soon as it is dry or it will become brittle.

BORAX AND SAND

Borax is a powder which is best mixed with a fine, dry sand. As a rule, mix three parts of chemical to two parts of sand. Use the combination in the same way as for silica gel but wait at least 10 days before checking to see if the flowers and leaves are dry. Desiccants are good for use on: roses, peonies, zinnias, delphiniums, gentians, hellebores, small dahlias, larkspurs, orchids and narcissi.

Above: A basket shape, bought from a florist's supplier, is decorated with dried chili peppers, ivy leaves, a selection of leaves in fall tones and a small white bloom for a contrasting color. Opposite: Potpourri sachets tied with ribbon are a pretty, fragrant gift idea.

Other ideas for dried material include:

small arrangements created in vases or country-style baskets; decorative wreaths to hang in living rooms, kitchens, dining rooms and bedrooms; posies as presents; lavender or potpourri sachets to hang in closets or place in drawers to ward off musty smells, or to hang on a doorknob to greet guests on arrival.

FINISHING TECHNIQUES

MANY OF THE FLOWERS and bunches of leaves you have chosen to dry will need to be wired to make up for a shortness of stem, or to make the arrangement less fragile. Stub wire is ideal for this, as it is flexible and strong, and rose wire is excellent to bind. Use gutta-percha tape to disguise the wire.

Wiring a flower head is easy if you follow these instructions carefully:

1 Cut off flower head, leaving about 1 inch of stem.

2 Hold stub wire so it touches the base of the flower and is next to stem. Wind a length of fine rose wire around stub wire and stem. Wind down the stub wire for about 3 inches. Cut rose wire and fold in carefully.

3 Hold flower head upside down, place the end of gutta-percha tape behind the stem on the diagonal. Keeping the tape taut, wind this down in a spiral to cover the wires. Cut it and neatly fold in the ends.

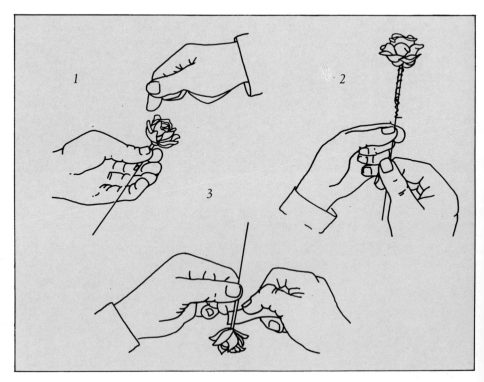

WIRING BUNCHES

Use a lengthy piece of medium-gauge stub wire and place it next to the stem ends. About 2 inches up the stem, bend the wire down behind the group of stems so that this becomes a short end reaching as far as the end of the bunch of stems. Continue winding the long end of the wire down over the stems and short wire, using what is left to make an extension to the flower stems.

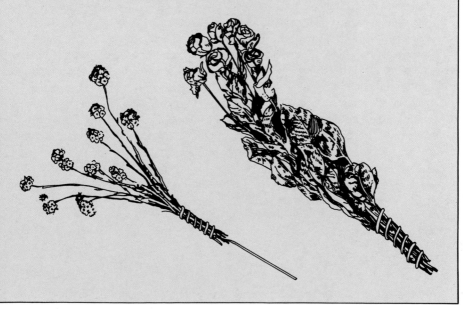

MAKING A WREATH

The wreath was one of the earliest home decorating traditions, especially popular at festive times such as Thanksgiving and Christmas. There are a variety of bases and shapes to choose from for a wreath. The base you decide upon will dictate the style of wreath. You may decide to decorate only a small part of a circle or heart, leaving the beauty of the base to show through. Many of the grape or honeysuckle vines are especially attractive with a cleverly placed decoration and bow.

BASES FOR A WREATH

Buy a wire frame from a florist or ready-made straw shape; use grapevine, honeysuckle, or wisteria vine.

If you want to try your hand at a vine wreath, be sure to make it while the vine is still green. Strip off the leaves and make a circle of several lengths, holding them securely at one end and twisting each length over the other. When you are happy with the shape, tuck in the ends and glue these in place. You can cover the join with dried flowers and herbs and perhaps a bow.

You can make your own wire shapes using thick wire (as in a coat hanger). Bend the wire into the required shape, bind it with thick twine and cover it with dried material.

Once you have decided upon the shape and style of base, choose which colors of flowers, herbs and leaves you want for the wreath. Pale pink, cream and pale blue make a lovely combination, as does a selection of gold, yellow and cream.

Decide from which point the wreath will hang and arrange your design on a symmetrical basis from that point. Insert stems into the wreath base, making sure they are secure. Glue the material into place if it does not have a stem.

Ideal plants for wreaths include yarrow, lavender, rose buds, sea lavender, goldenrod, statice, celosia, small flowers of chives, marjoram, mint and sage.

Dried seed pods and berries are especially effective on country-style wreaths.

PLANNING ARRANGEMENTS

There are few rules for creating an arrangement, but design factors must be taken into consideration.

Where is the arrangement to sit in the room? That will dictate the size and shape. What colors and textures are in the immediate environment? These factors will guide you in choosing the textures and colors of the dried flowers and plants to be used. It is always best to be guided by nature. By studying natural forms where, amazingly, everything is almost always in correct proportion, you will begin to develop an "eye" for arrangements. You will soon recognize when flowers look squashed and unsightly in the wrong-shaped container.

Colors close to each other in the color spectrum mix well. As a rule, arrangements containing a mixture of red, orange, yellow and cream will look wonderful; shades of blue (statice, deep blue larkspur and sea holly);

Opposite: A collection of hand-decorated wreaths brightens up this country kitchen.

pink, cream and pale yellow (pink silene, cream statice and yellow roses); red, rust and orange (red roses, rust or orange helichrysum); or contrasting combinations of blue, yellow and green can also be successful (cornflower, yellow helichrysum and feathery acacia.)

Do not be afraid to try your own combinations, but it is usually best to choose shades of a similar intensity.

Leaves with texture are excellent as a foil to the beauty of flowers. Try to overlap each leaf slightly so that each casts a shadow on the surrounding flowers and leaves.

Each dried flower has individual beauty, so look for a range of textures through from soft, fluffy plants to those with thick, lustrous petals, and even leaves with strong veins.

Each textural detail helps to make the final arrangement a special achievement. Finding the right container is important, as is the preparation before arranging.

IDEAS FOR CONTAINERS

Vases of various heights and shapes; ordinary glass containers like jars, tumblers or even a goldfish bowl; a wooden salad bowl that has outlived its use; any painted wooden box; baskets, tin buckets, old saucepans (particularly if these are copper); antique pewter mugs, and terra cotta pots.

For the preparation of a basket you will need dry sphagnum moss, florist's styrofoam and cellophane tape.

1   Press the styrofoam into the base of basket.

If necessary, cut it to shape.

2   Place a second block of styrofoam, cut in the form of a small mound, on top. It ought to show about 2 inches above the basket rim.

3   Tape into position by inserting narrow tape through the basket rim and across the styrofoam to slip through the cane on the other side. Cover this mound completely with moss.

4   Low, flat, florist's saucer-shapes are best with a dry styrofoam block shaped to fit, stuck on a prong attached to the saucer with plastic putty. Again, cover the block with moss.

5   Most spherical vases benefit from having a loose ball of chicken wire carefully inserted and stretched until it feels firmly in place.

6   For Christmas tree decorations, buy one of the many round styrofoam shapes available from florist's suppliers; there are also cone shapes suitable for dried table arrangements. Cover these with moss, dried flower heads and herbs, place the arrangement near a color coordinating candle casting a gentle glow, and you have created a magic setting.

HANGING UP

Whether it is a bunch of dried material, a wreath, or a swag above a fireplace, anything that hangs must have a loop from which it can be hung.

Opposite: Many brides like to have a memento of the wedding day. One of the easiest ways to do this is to air-dry the bridal bouquet.

It is important that the loop is hidden, so consider its design carefully.

A popular way of making a loop to hang a wreath is as follows:

- Cover a piece of fairly strong stub wire with gutta-percha tape and twist a circle in the middle.
- Push the ends of the wire into the wreath base.
- Pull them back under the frame, which pulls the circle towards the frame.
- Then push each wire end into the frame on either side to secure it in position (see illustration.)

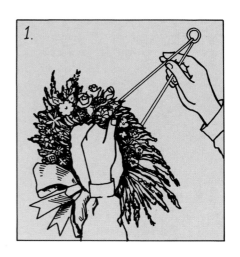

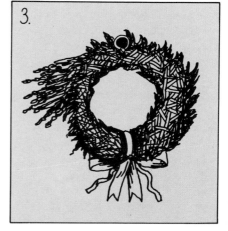

Try making a plaited raffia bow for a country look, as follows:

- Plait a good length of raffia strands, making the ends neat.

- Form a figure eight and bind this where the two ends cross over, using stub wire, leaving long ends (as on a ribbon bow.)
- Attach bow to bunch with raffia twine.

Opposite: A bouquet of dried flowers similar to the one shown opposite the title page but made up in a different color scheme and tied with a soft green moiré taffeta bow.

The completed project is an attractive gift box – a personal treasure chest for precious items such as old love letters, jewels, ribbons, buttons and badges.

BEGINNER'S PROJECT

Designed by Clare Ryan of Modern Wildflowers

BEFORE ATTEMPTING to make this attractive gift box, read through the instructions carefully and gather all the materials together. Think through the processes involved. Also think about the color combinations you prefer – this one is in cream, pink and lavender. Have confidence in your creativity – and exercise patience. You will be pleasantly surprised at how easy this project is – and you will be delighted with the result.

A selection of boxes in different shapes.

Some of the items you will need for this project, from left: bunch of small roses, statice, laven

For this project you will need the following items:

1	large round, square or rectangular cardboard box
1	roll of paper twist
6	ivy leaves
6	lavender heads wired into a bunch
10	nigella (love-in-a-mist) heads
6	small roses
	glue gun
	shears
	statice

Take the lid off the box and place it to one side. Unravel the paper twist, placing one end on the inside rim at the center of the box. Glue this into position. Bring it under the box and up to turn into the inside rim. Cut the paper twist and glue it into position. Repeat the same steps for the lid.

With the paper twist, cut a length of about 12 inches and unravel. Twist it around to make a rosette for the center of the box lid. Place it on the paper twist strip already in place, and glue it. That is the center of the design.

Place the ivy and rose leaves around each side of the rosette. Glue these into place. Position three roses on each side of the rosette and glue them. On each side of the roses, add lavender and statice. Then add two clusters of four nigella heads, one either side of the rosette.

Make sure all stems are hidden under the central rosette, and use the glue gun carefully and sparingly.

The result is a charming gift for family or friends, for birthdays, Mother's Day, or a special thought for someone in hospital.

*This is a smaller box than the completed one shown on page 42, and was photographed to
illustrate the question of proportion. The paper twist, ivy leaves and the first rose heads are in
place. The leaves are too large for the size of box and the roses are dominating the design.
Should you wish to make a smaller box, choose small, dried material that will not take up most of
the lid. Try lavender or cornflower heads and sprays of baby's breath.
Remember to keep a sense of proportion in each of your designs.*

INDEX